472379

NEWNES' ART
LIBRARY

BENOZZO GOZZOLI

MICHELE·PALEOLOGO
ROBED·AS·ONE·OF·THE
MAGI·FROM·THE·FRESCO
BY·GOZZOLI·IN·THE·RI
CCARDI·PALACE·FLORENCE

Photo. Brogi.

BENOZZO GOZZOLI

LONDON · GEORGE · NEWNES · LIMITED
SOVTHAMPTON · STREET · STRAND · W·C
NEW·YORK: FREDERICK·WARNE·&·CO·36·EAST·22nd·ST.

BALLANTYNE PRESS
LONDON & EDINBURGH

CONTENTS

LIST OF ILLUSTRATIONS

LIST OF ILLUSTRATIONS—*continued.*

BENOZZO GOZZOLI

BY HUGH STOKES

ENOZZO GOZZOLI flourished in the beginning of one of the most interesting periods in the artistic development of the world. The era was one of transition, and Gozzoli lived long enough to see the old aims and ideals of mediæval Christendom gradually submerged beneath the fascinating teaching of a bygone civilisation. If an arbitrary date can be accepted as roughly indicating the beginning of the Renaissance, namely, 1453, when Constantinople was conquered by Mahomet and the Turks, we find that the artist passed the greater portion of his existence under those novel conditions of life and thought which permeated Italy during the latter half of the fifteenth century. Gozzoli was a true child of his age, and his works reflect the spirit of the early Renaissance in a very marked degree.

Benozzo di Lese (the surname of Gozzoli being added after his death) was born in Florence, either in 1420 or 1424. The first date is that given by himself and generally accepted as correct. The alternative year has been extracted from an income paper filled up by his father in 1470. At that time no better environment than Florence could be found for the education of an artist. Of all the countries of the globe Italy was the most cultured, and of the many cities in that " garden of the world " Florence was indisputably first in scholarship, science, philosophy, and the arts. Her supremacy was never challenged, and the inhabitants of the town on the banks of the Arno became famous for the quickness of their intelligence and their enthusiastic love for the beautiful. Florence became a second Athens, and the Florentines of the Renaissance have many points of resemblance to the Greeks before the fall of their power.

The arts were encouraged by the people themselves, and the skill of architects and sculptors rapidly became visible throughout the city.

BENOZZO GOZZOLI

Arnolfo's cathedral, vaulted over in 1364, was crowned by Brunelleschi's massive dome in 1446, after twenty years of labour. Donatello had commenced his great career. Giotto's campanile had already become a well-known landmark, and Ghiberti was engaged upon the colossal bronze gates of the Baptistry. It is not difficult to recreate the chief architectural features of Florence in the days of Gozzoli's youth. The artist himself has supplied us with portraits of the busy but effeminate citizens who crowded its streets.

According to one authority, Gozzoli was apprenticed to Lorenzo Ghiberti, and worked for three years upon the great gates, an example of the facility with which Italian artists were able to turn from one branch of the crafts to another. About this time Gozzoli painted an altar-piece for the company of S. Mark, and a panel for the church of S. Frediano. Both of these works have been lost.

A far greater influence upon the young painter has yet to be mentioned. In the convent at Fiesole, and afterwards in Florence itself, lived and worked Fra Angelico, type to this day of the Christian artist who strives towards an ideal of spirituality and faith rather than any high standard of creative imagination or technical workmanship. Modern critics scoff at many of the details of the monk's private life as related by Vasari. There is, however, no good reason to disbelieve their authenticity, and personal legend, handed down from generation to generation by word of mouth, is far more worthy of credence than the blind speculations of the historian. Gozzoli was the favourite pupil of Fra Angelico, and some characteristics of his master are worth recapitulation. " He would not follow the ways of the world, but lived purely and holily, and was a great friend of the poor. . . . He might have been rich, but did not care about it, saying that true riches are nothing else than being content with little. . . . He did not esteem dignities, affirming that he sought no other dignity than to escape hell and attain to Paradise. . . . He was most kind and sober, keeping himself free from all worldly tire, often saying that he who represents the things of Christ should always live with Christ. He was never seen in anger, and had a way of admonishing his friends with smiles. He was most humble and modest. Some say he would never take up his pencil until he had first made supplication, and he never made a crucifix but he was bathed in tears." The pupil was fortunate with such a master. An individuality of this powerful type must have had tremendous influence upon the impressionable nature of a boy. The little we know of Gozzoli's personality proves that he never quite forgot the lessons, both material and moral, inculcated by the saintly Dominican.

When the monastery of S. Mark was given by the Pope to the monks in 1436, Fra Angelico and his brethren moved from their cells at Fiesole into the city of Florence. It is probable that Gozzoli entered his service as a pupil about this time. It is not unlikely that he assisted in the decoration of the new buildings raised by Cosimo de' Medici. He is said to have visited Rome. Vasari writes that Gozzoli painted the chapel of the Cesarini, in the church of Aracoeli, with the history of S. Anthony of Padua, and Cavalcaselle admits that the frescoes reveal the hand of the young Florentine. In 1447 Fra Angelico agreed to paint a new chapel, that of the Madonna of S. Brizio, in the recently completed cathedral of Orvieto. This he undertook to do with the aid of his pupil Gozzoli, and his two assistants, Giovanni d'Antonio and Giacomo da Poli. The monk was to receive under the terms of the contract two hundred gold ducats a year, Gozzoli seven ducats each month and the assistants three. Twenty lire monthly were added for board and lodging, a sufficiency of bread and wine, and all the materials for the painting. Fra Angelico seems to have sketched out the designs and left his assistants to complete, for soon after he journeyed to Rome, and does not appear to have revisited Orvieto. His death took place in 1455.

Gozzoli had now become his own master. His pupilage had ended, and he entered upon an independent career. Naturally the first thing he did was to apply to the council which controlled the works at Orvieto for permission to complete the unfinished labours of Fra Angelico. The council asked for examples of his skill, a request somewhat without reason, for the artist must have been at work in the cathedral for nearly eighteen months. More inexplicable still is the fact that Benozzo evidently failed to satisfy the council, for a few months later he settled in the little town of Montefalco. Committees we know are, at all times, difficult to please, and when several men act as a committee of taste they form an eccentric body liable to extraordinary and unintelligible action. Had Gozzoli not been in the prime of his life and art he would possibly have secured the commission.

However, at Montefalco he was extremely successful. In the church of S. Fortunato he painted a fresco, on the portal, of a Virgin and Child amongst saints and angels, an altar-piece representing the apotheosis of the saint, an Annunciation, and an altar-piece of S. Thomas receiving the girdle, now in the museum of the Lateran at Rome. This latter work, one of the best of his earlier achievements, was painted in the manner of his old master, and has, indeed, been assgned to Fra Angelico.

A more ambitious undertaking was entered into at the monastery of S. Francesco. Quoting those well-known critics Crowe and Cavalcaselle, Gozzoli " filled the hexagonal choir with a triple course of episodes from the life of S. Francis, copious adjuncts of saints in the ceiling and window, and portraits in medallions along the lower skirting of the principal subject and in the vaulting of the entrance arch. Scrolls held by angels in the pilasters of the entrance contain inscriptions from which it appears that Benozzo's patron was the Franciscan Jacopo di Montefalco, and that the whole choir was completed in 1452." These frescoes repay a careful examination, as the essentials of Gozzoli's talent are clearly displayed. He had learnt all that Fra Angelico could teach him. He possessed a respectable knowledge of the practice of perspective, and his figure drawing, though stiff and at times awkward, had not degenerated as it did in later examples. As one of his critics observes, his spirit is a religious and kindly one, natural in the pupil of such a master as Angelico. Some of the subjects in this series, notably *S. Francis supporting the Falling Church*, and *S. Francis expelling the Devils from Arezzo*, are reminiscent of Giotto, for whom Gozzoli evidently had much esteem. Here also we see for the first time indications of Gozzoli's love for children and animals. There are some delightful little boys in one corner of *S. Francis protected from his Father's Wrath*, and a most naturally drawn pouting child in the *Nativity*. The architecture forms an odd study. In the *Nativity* at Grezzo we have a curious and ugly mixture of early gothic and revived classic forms. The strongly marked classic pilasters with their elaborately floriated capitals clearly indicate the artistic ferment of the fifteenth century. The architectural details in Gozzoli's paintings are always interesting. In the building which S. Francis sees in his dream, and in the view of the town of Arezzo, the elevations are evidently based upon the artist's recollections of the Bargello and the Palazzo Vecchio at Florence.

Gozzoli remained in Montefalco until about 1456. He employed an assistant, Mesastris by name, and to this fact one may attribute the inferiority of the frescoes in the chapel of S. Jerome, the Madonna and saints on the wall, a crucifixion above, four evangelists in the ceiling, scenes from the life of S. Sebastian on the pilasters, and figures of saints in the vaulting of the entrance.

About this year Gozzoli painted a Madonna with saints for a church in Perugia. He then resettled in Florence, and was soon employed upon the decorations of the Medici palace, now known as the Palazzo Riccardi.

The story of the Medici family forms an integral part of the history of Italy. One of the richest banking houses of the Middle Ages, they speedily attained an actual, though not at first an official, power in the government of Florence which placed the family in a position of supreme importance. Cosimo de Medici was not only a business man with genius, but a most munificent supporter of arts and letters. And although the characteristics of the family gradually changed, until the dominance of the race was lost and the last head of the Medici faded out of history like a senile old man imperceptibly wasting away from the life around him, few members of the family seem to have been without this hereditary affection for art and artists. The paintings in the Riccardi Palace thus remain not only a monument to the talent of their creator, but also a memorial of the taste and discernment of the early Medicis.

Had Gozzoli not painted the walls of the Medici chapel but little of his fame would have survived until the present day. As it is, in the procession of the kings which slowly winds round the walls of the little chapel we have one of the most fascinating mural decorations in the world. The exterior of the palace is decidedly gloomy, with a massive cornice casting a perpetual frown across the upper storeys of the building, and a crude and heavy rustication of the ground floor which gives an impression of tremendous strength, an impression heightened by the heavily barred windows. Half palace, half fortress, prepared to successfully meet and repel any attacks from a fickle rabble, it is difficult to imagine that it houses such a gem as the chapel of the Medici.

The chapel is exceedingly small, about twenty feet by twenty-five. At the end of the seventeenth century it was proposed to demolish the whole, but, by good fortune, only a corner was cut away, giving the plan a somewhat irregular appearance. Originally the chapel possessed one door and no window, and it is suggested that Gozzoli worked upon the walls before the roof was added. A barbarian at some later period destroyed a portion of the painting for an additional doorway, removed the altar-piece, which was the culminating point of the procession, and inserted the window which now lights the chamber. Otherwise the walls are exactly as Gozzoli left them, the colours hardly unstained by the four centuries which have elapsed since they were fresh. The artist speaks of these colours in a letter which has escaped destruction. "My dearest friend," he writes to Piero de' Medici, who had succeeded his father Cosimo, "I informed your Magnificence in a previous letter that I am in need of fifty florins, and begged you to advance them to me, for now is the time to buy corn and many other things that I want, whereby I shall save, and get out of a load of care. I also reminded you to send to Venice for some ultramarine, for in the course of this week one wall will be finished, and for the other I shall need ultramarine. The brocades and other things can then be finished, as well as the figures." The paintings have been preserved so well that we can study the figures, "the brocades and other things," almost as well as if the painter had laid them on a day before. This cannot be said of all the work of Gozzoli ; the frescoes in the Campo Santo at Pisa, for instance, have suffered severely.

Although the *Procession of the Magi* is a subject nominally belonging to sacred art, the religious spirit is singularly lacking in this fantastic cavalcade. Gozzoli did not trouble to depict eastern monarchs with swarthy skins and outlandish retinues. He selected his types from the crowd around him, and, for the vanity of his own generation and the benefit of its descendants, drew in a realistic manner the features of all the prominent Florentines of 1460. One of the most striking figures is that of the youthful Lorenzo the Magnificent, who became head of the Medici family in 1469, at the age of twenty. Amongst the horsemen who follow in his train is Benozzo himself. (The head is

BENOZZO GOZZOLI

full face, the third row from the bottom of the picture, counting the fourth full face from the left of the frame.) Each character in the whole procession is a portrait of some dependent or supporter of the great house which ruled Florence for nearly three hundred years.

For its fascination the painting has no equal. This glorious pageant solemnly makes its way towards the manger in which rests the Holy Babe. Rocks, mountains, woods, plains watered by rippling streams, all are depicted with a minute realism. We receive a brilliant and true impression of Florentine pomp at a most exciting epoch in European history.

The Italian, as he shook off the chains of mediævalism and emerged into the freer atmosphere of the Renaissance, was a curious being, controlled by many opposing currents. In this painting we can study the type of man who supported the Medici family against the Pazzi. The story is a vivid illustration of the interest of existence during the fifteenth century to Italians who interested themselves in politics, or even municipal government, which was, in fact, synonymous. In 1478 the Pazzi conspired to take the lives of Lorenzo and his younger brother, Guiliano, as they attended mass in the cathedral church of the city. The Elevation of the Host was selected as a convenient signal for the attack. But even the conspirators could not nerve themselves to the perpetration of murder during the most solemn and impressive moment of the Mass. Old bottles can seldom satisfactorily take new wine, and the free thought of the Renaissance could not immediately conquer centuries of ecclesiastical tradition. A priest seized the dagger. Lorenzo escaped into the sacristy with a flesh wound in his thigh, leaving his brother a corpse on the steps of the sanctuary. Popular feeling was with the Medici, and an ugly vengeance sought out the partisans of the Pazzi clan. The archbishop himself, in his episcopal robes, swung from the window of a Florentine palace, victim to the wrath of the Medici. Then followed pontifical thunder, not against the men who had shed blood in a consecrated building, but against those who had executed an assassin. Pope Sixtus IV. excommunicated the whole city for hanging his bishop. In Gozzoli's paintings we are able to see the actors in sanguinary dramas of this description, which culminated under Lorenzo the Magnificent in the unparalleled ferocities of the sack of Volterra.

Benozzo Gozzoli had too tender a soul to depict such scenes. Even when he ventured upon a martyrdom we have a very placid and untroubled saint. In the procession of the kings he drew a careful picture of what could be seen from any window in Florence when one prince paid a visit of state to another. We have historical mention of such a visit (some years after the chapel was completed), when Duke Galeazzo Maria Sforza of Milan and his wife Bona of Savoy came to see the Medici in Florence. They arrived attended by the whole court, writes the historian of the Renaissance, John Addington Symonds ; bodyguards on horse and foot, ushers, pages, falconers, grooms, kennel varlets, and huntsmen. Omitting the mere baggage service, their train counted two thousand horses. Florence was crowded with nobles and courtiers, and luxury and prodigal expenditure abounded. Masked balls and tournaments succeeded each other in profusion. As we read the words of the historian the procession of the Magi rises before our eyes, and we see Italian history as illustrated by a contemporary.

The sanctuary of the chapel is adorned by groups of angels. In the centre stood the lost altar-piece, which represented the *Nativity*. These delightful compositions display the influence of Fra Angelico in a marked degree. But the temperaments of the Dominican monk and Benozzo Gozzoli bear no comparison. Fra Angelico painted his angels with a spiritual exaltation Gozzoli never felt. Gozzoli painted hard matter-of-fact portraits, charming portraits, it is admitted, but possessing little of the idealism of the older painter. The yeast of the Renaissance spirit was beginning to work. Fra Angelico was uninfluenced by the new movement ; he was too old. Gozzoli was younger and more impressionable. He moved about in a world which was openly weighing classical ethics against the teaching of the church. It required a man of extremely strong personality and most decided ideas to remain unsettled by such influences. There is an odd story told of a young patriot who had been sentenced to death for a political offence. An artist (Lippo Lippi) sat with his friend throughout the night previous to the execution. No fear of death beset the youth. He accepted, evidently with faith, all the consolations religion could offer. But throughout his conversation he continued to mention Brutus, to whom he likened his own career. He was a hero as the Roman had been. During his last hours Christian teaching was almost forgotten in the glory of imagining that he had followed in the footsteps of a noble pagan exemplar. It is idle to expect that in a community so dominated by classical learning and tradition, the painters and poets could remain subject to much deep religious zeal and impulse. Indeed, nowhere can such feeling be discovered in the works of Gozzoli.

Benozzo was famous for the rapidity with which he worked, and the chapel of the Riccardi Palace was finished in 1460. He then painted some panel pictures. The larger example in the National Gallery was probably executed about this time. In 1464, according to one authority, he was enrolled amongst the doctors and apothecaries of Florence, but why amongst the doctors does not appear clear. About this same year he settled in the town of S. Gimignano, where he worked under the patronage of Domenico Strambi, also known as Parisinus, by reason of his long stay in the capital town of France. Here Gozzoli painted above the altar of S. Sebastian in the church of S. Agostino, a picture of the titular martyr clothed in a long mantle so held by a number of angels as to shelter a crowd of supplicants. The Saviour and the Mother implore the mercy of the Almighty, who launches forth thunderbolts which are intercepted by the Saint. The subject, which some critics consider trivial, was intended as a pictorial realisation of the intervention of S. Sebastian to preserve S. Gimignano from the plague which raged throughout the town in 1464. The commission did not excite Gozzoli to any high flights of imagination. Possibly his faith in the power of the saints had been impaired by the new learning. Certainly the Father is depicted in an essentially Olympean manner. The crucified Saviour beneath, with four adoring saints, and twelve medallions at each side, is the votive gift of Domenico Strambi, whose kneeling presence in miniature form in the foreground is declared by the words F.D.M.P. (" frater dominicus Magister Parisiensis.")

In attempting to reproduce the personality of Gozzoli we would like to imagine him as a man of much pluck and endurance. It is evident that he enjoyed a big work. During his past career he had painted the large frescoes depicting the life of S. Francis at Montefalco. The Procession of the Magi at the Riccardi Palace was of considerable size, and its environment subjected it to the severe criticism of the whole of the country. Now, with a light heart, Gozzoli commenced to cover the choir of the church of S. Agostino at S. Gemignano with a triple course of episodes from the life of Saint Augustine, from the time when he entered the grammar school until his burial. That he undertook them with a light heart is unquestionable, for the first fresco, *The Entrance of Saint Augustine into the Grammar School*, vibrates with life and activity. It contains all the movement of the opening scene of a play. Gozzoli was untroubled by the miraculous power of saints, and his compositions are painted throughout in a purely secular spirit. His work is, however, glowing with humanity. He loves to paint animals and children. Naturally children abound in the grammar school, and one unfortunate child has become immortalised. The architectural vista is exceptionally interesting, the detail being again strongly classical.

There is no necessity to follow the story of the frescoes. In the *Departure of Saint Augustine for Milan* we have a typical open-air composition in which Gozzoli excelled. The angels with the scroll are said to be by Gozzoli's assistant, Guisto d'Andrea. *Saint Augustine teaching in Rome* is praised by Crowe and Cavalcaselle as being one of the best, a remark we can hardly agree with. There is an entertaining dog in the foreground which appears to take a keener interest in the Saint's lecture upon rhetoric than many of the other students, some of whom are plainly bored. *The Death of Saint Monica* is notable not so much for the saint herself as for the charming episode of the children in the foreground. One must ask pardon for suggesting that Gozzoli, as he designed these frescoes, had at least one friendship (if not many) amongst the children of S. Gemignano. In his frescoes he inserted little commentaries for the benefit of that lovable individual, the bad child. In the first fresco we have a vivid impression of what undoubtedly happens to the child who neglects his tasks, or who defies authority. In this design we note the dangers incidental to teasing dogs. The *Saint Augustine with the Monks of Monte Pisano* contains one of the most exquisitely natural children the painter ever drew. Across the centuries we are able to recreate the personality of this peaceful artist, and by these little pictures of children and animals (two communities in our involved and degenerate world which retain their pristine innocence and beauty much as the Almighty created them) we are able to say that Benozzo Gozzoli was a lovable man of pure and gentle soul.

Two remaining frescoes should be noted. *The Ecstasy of Saint Augustine* is prosaic, in fact decidedly unecstatic. Fra Angelico would have revelled in a subject which has left Gozzoli untouched. The *Death of Saint Augustine* is very successful in its grouping. The whole series has much life.

The next works Gozzoli executed were chiefly altar-pieces. We are told that he painted the martrydom of S. Sebastian between the portals of the church of S. Gemignano, and a crucified Saviour and saints in the court of the Convent of Monte Oliveto. He also painted some Madonnas, and a Marriage of S. Catherine for churches in S. Gemignano and Terni, and he decorated a chapel on the outskirts of Certaldo. His assistant, Guisto d'Andrea, had a share in several of these commissions, probably being responsible for the greater part of the tabernacle at S. Chiara of Castel Fiorentino. In 1467 Gozzoli restored Lippo Memmi's frescoes in the Palazzo del Podesta at S. Gemignano, and in the summer of that year he wrote to Lorenzo de' Medici begging him to assist Giovanni di Mugello, who had been accused of stealing some sheets from a monastery at Certaldo. Gozzoli was evidently one of those amiable men who would do anything to help a friend in trouble, even when the friend had gone so far as to steal sheets.

Towards the close of 1468 Gozzoli commenced his last and greatest work. The frescoes in the Campo Santo at Pisa number twenty-four in all. Although he worked upon them for sixteen years it was probably not a continuous labour, and local tradition (which is seldom exactly true) affirms that he was only two years over the whole. This can hardly be correct, for, from documentary evidence, we know that the first fresco, *Noah and his Family*, engaged him during nine months.

In these frescoes, as in the previous ones, the religious spirit is wanting, though the subjects are selected from sacred writ. Many of the figures are classical in pose and drapery (especially those in the vintage scene). Gozzoli's technical method, as Crowe and Cavalcaselle point out, on wall as well as on panel, is simple. In flesh he paints his shadows grey, with a warm general liquid tint for light by their side, and he stripples the whole with red. In draperies he places the lights and shadows with a copious and high surface over a general local colour. In these frescoes vast quantities of colour have scaled off, and the stippling has frequently become black. Gozzoli's chief assistant was Zanobi Macchiavelli.

The artist received payment for the last fresco, that of *Solomon receiving the Queen of Sheba*, in 1485. His industry had been incessant, for he not only painted many panel pictures for the churches around Pisa, but accepted commissions at a distance. In 1480 in an income paper now in the archives at Venice, he stated that he possessed land and houses at Florence, and a house in Pisa, where he lived with his brother Domenico and the joint families. The grateful Pisans presented him with a tomb in the Campo Santo he had decorated so magnificently, and the date inscribed thereon has often been taken as the date of his death. This is not so, and the exact year is doubtful. He was at work in 1497, and probably died in the following year. No better epitaph could be found than the final paragraph in Vasari's short biography : " Being at length worn out by years and toil, he went to his true rest at the age of seventy-eight in the city of Pisa, in a house in Carraia di S. Francesco, which he had bought during his long stay there. This house he left to his daughter when dying, and amid the universal mourning of the city he was honourably buried in the Campo Santo, with this epitaph, which may still be read :

HIC TUMULUS EST BENOTII FLORENTINI,
QUI PROXIME HAS PINXIT HISTORIAS :
HUNC SIBI PISANOR, DONAVIT HUMANITAS
MCCCCLXXVIII.

Benozzo always lived most temperately, and like a good Christian, spending his whole life in worthy employments, thus winning the esteem of the Pisans for his virtues as well as by his abilities."

Vasari gives a criticism which is to some extent just, and its quaintness calls for quotation. " He was of great invention, very fertile in animals, in perspective, in landscapes and in ornament. He produced so much during his life that it is plain that he cared for no other occupation. And, although compared to others who surpassed him in drawing he was not very excellent, yet the amount of work he did placed him ahead of all his contemporaries, because, in the multitude of his works, some turned out well." Vasari forgot when he wrote this bitter last line that an artist is always judged by the best work he produces, not by the worst. Gozzoli's claim to rank with the great artists of his country may be disputed, but amongst the painters of the early Renaissance he must stand as one of the most talented and certainly the most fascinating.

LIST OF THE PRINCIPAL WORKS OF BENOZZO GOZZOLI

ITALY

FLORENCE

PALAZZO RICCARDI (Chapel of the Medici).

THE JOURNEY OF THE MAGI. (Fresco.)
"It is said that the altar-piece of the Riccardi Palace is in the Munich Gallery. This is not so. It may, however, be in the private collection of the King of Bavaria."—Crowe and Cavalcaselle.

GROUPS OF ANGELS.

UFFIZI GALLERY.

AN ALTAR-PIECE.
In the centre a Pietà, on the sides Saint John and the Magdalen, the Virgin and the Child betrothed to Saint Catharine, also Saint Anthony and Saint Benedict. Originally in the Convent of Santa Croce, Florence, etc.

MILAN

PINACOTECA DI BRERA.

SAINT DOMINIC REVIVING A CHILD KILLED BY A HORSE.

PERUGIA

ACCADEMIA DELLE BELLE ARTI.

VIRGIN AND CHILD.
Between SS. Peter, John the Baptist, Jerome, and Paul, with a predella representing the Resurrection, with SS. Thomas, Laurence, Sebastian, and Bernard.

PISA

Frescoes in the CAMPO SANTO.

THE CURSE OF HAM.

BUILDING OF THE TOWER OF BABEL.

xvii

BENOZZO GOZZOLI

ADORATION OF THE MAGI.

THE ANNUNCIATION.

THE VINTAGE, AND THE DRUNKENNESS OF NOAH.

ABRAHAM AND LOT IN EGYPT.

ABRAHAM'S VICTORY.

ABRAHAM AND HAGAR ; ABRAHAM AND THE WORSHIPPERS OF BAAL.

DESTRUCTION OF SODOM, AND ESCAPE OF LOT.

THE SACRIFICE OF ISAAC.

THE MARRIAGE OF REBECCA.

BIRTH OF JACOB AND ESAU.

THE MARRIAGE OF JACOB AND RACHEL, AND JACOB'S DREAM.

CORONATION OF THE VIRGIN (over the window).

MEETING OF JACOB AND ESAU, AND RAPE OF DINAH.

THE INNOCENCE OF JOSEPH.

JOSEPH MADE KNOWN TO HIS BROTHERS.

INFANCY OF MOSES, AND THE FIRST MIRACLE OF MOSES.

PASSAGE OF THE RED SEA.

THE TABLES OF THE LAW.

AARON'S ROD, AND THE BRAZEN SERPENT.

FALL OF JERICHO, AND DAVID AND GOLIATH.

THE VISIT OF THE QUEEN OF SHEBA TO KING SOLOMON.

The following frescoes have been obliterated :

THE DESTRUCTION OF DATHAN AND ABIRAM.

THE DEATH OF AARON.

A number of designs by Gozzoli for this series were formerly in the possession of Don José Madrazo at Madrid, who bought them at Pisa. They had, however, all been retouched.

The drawing of the Queen of Sheba, now in the Accademia at Pisa, is probably a copy from the fresco and not an original design.

ACCADEMIA DELLE BELLE ARTI.

CARTOON FOR FRESCO OF SOLOMON AND THE QUEEN OF SHEBA.
See note to the Campo Santo frescoes.

HEAD OF DANTE.
This is doubtful.

VIRGIN AND CHILD WITH SAINTS.
Originally in San Benedetto a Ripa d'Arno.

THE CONCEPTION.

Montefalco

Church of San Francesco.

Frescoes in the Choir.

SCENES FROM THE LIFE OF SAINT FRANCIS.

A triple course of twelve scenes from the life of Saint Francis, five medallions of illustrious Dominicans, and portraits of Petrarch, Dante, and Giotto (sometimes said to be a portrait of Gozzoli), besides numerous figures of saints and angels.

The scenes from the life of Saint Francis fill four sides of the choir, beginning on the lower course of the nearest left side with his birth, and ending with his death, in the lunette of the nearest side to the right. The order of the subjects is as follows:

Lower Course.

1. THE BIRTH, AND THE EPISODE OF THE CLOAK THROWN ON THE GROUND FOR SAINT FRANCIS TO WALK UPON.

2. SAINT FRANCIS GIVES HIS DRESS TO THE POOR; HE SEES A PALACE IN A DREAM.

3. HE IS PROTECTED FROM HIS FATHER'S ANGER BY THE BISHOP OF ASSISI.

4. MEETING OF SS. FRANCIS AND DOMINIC; WITH THE VIRGIN WARDING OFF THE THUNDERBOLTS.

Second Course also from Left to Right.

5. SAINT FRANCIS SUPPORTING THE FALLING CHURCH.

6. SAINT FRANCIS EXPELLING DEVILS FROM AREZZO.

7. SAINT FRANCIS AND THE SPARROWS.
Saint Francis is blessing the donors Jacopo di Montefalco and Marco, who kneel before him.

8. SAINT FRANCIS AND THE CAVALIER OF CELANO.

Lunettes.

9. THE NATIVITY AT GREGGIO.

10. SAINT FRANCIS BEFORE THE SOLDAN.

11. SAINT FRANCIS RECEIVING THE STIGMATA.

12. DEATH OF SAINT FRANCIS.
The saints in the vaulting are SS. Francis in Glory, Anthony, Catharine, Bernardin, Rosa of Vilerbo, and Louis.

Church of San Francesco, chapel of Saint Jerome.

A FRESCO ON THE WALL OF THE MADONNA AND CHILD.

The Crucifixion above, the four Evangelists in the ceiling, scenes from the life of Saint Sebastian on the pilasters, and various figures of saints and angels in the vaulting of the entrance.

This Madonna and Child is sometimes described as an altar-piece, with incidents from the life of Saint Jerome on either side. It is suggested that the vault and arch are probably painted by Pietro da Foligno.

CHURCH OF SAN FORTUNATO (outside Montefalco, on the road to Trevi).

The greater part of this Church appears to have been painted by Gozzoli. Crowe and Cavalcaselle mention the following works :

VIRGIN AND CHILD.
Above the portal, injured by the scaling of the dresses.

AN APOTHEOSIS OF SAINT FORTUNATO.
By the altar. All but the head of the Saint repainted by a restorer of the eighteenth century.

AN ANNUNCIATION, IN FRESCO.
The Virgin and Child with an Angel (dated 1450).

TERNI

CHURCH OF SAN FRANCESCO, CHAPEL OF THE RUSTICI FAMILY.
MARRIAGE OF SAINT CATHARINE.
Painted in 1466.

ORVIETO

CATHEDRAL, CHAPEL OF SAN BRIZIO.

Kugler, in the " Handbook of Painting," discovers the hand of Gozzoli in the figures of the Apostles and Martyrs which form a portion of the Glory in the Last Judgment by Fra Angelico on the roof of the chapel.

THE CHOIRS OF BLESSED SPIRITS.
Ranged according to hierarchic order on compartments of the vault are also ascribed to Gozzoli.

CERTALDO

CHAPEL OF THE GUISTIZIATI (at the foot of the Ponte dell' Agliena, on the outskirts of Certaldo).

A small edifice enclosing a tabernacle painted on all its sides, with a deposition from the Cross inside, the Crucifixion, and martyrdom of Saint Sebastian outside.
The deposition contains eleven figures : sides of tabernacle,

SS. Anthony Abbot, James the Elder, John the Baptist, and another. On the vaulting, the Eternal and four Evangelists. On the face of the arch, the Annunciation.

Castel Fiorentino

A Tabernacle in San Chiara.

VIRGIN AND CHILD BETWEEN SAINT PAUL AND OTHER SAINTS.
In the vaulting are the Evangelists and doctors of the church. In this work Gozzoli was probably helped by Guisto.

Meleto (near Castel Fiorentino)

VIRGIN AND CHILD WITH SAINTS.
Near the altar.

DEATH, BURIAL, AND ASCENSION OF THE VIRGIN.

GIFT OF THE MIRACULOUS GIRDLE TO SAINT THOMAS.
These frescoes are signed and dated 1484.

Volterra

The Cathedral, chapel of the Virgin.

A fresco forming the background to figures representing the Adoration of the Magi.

Legoli (between Pontedera and Volterra)

Chapel of Monsignor della Fanteria.

CHRIST CRUCIFIED, VIRGIN AND CHILD AND SAINTS, AND THE ANNUNCIATION.
This attribution is doubtful.

San Gimignano

Church of San Agostino.

Choir.

THE PRINCIPAL EVENTS IN THE LIFE OF SAINT AUGUSTINE.
These frescoes were painted in 1465 in seventeen compartments on the walls of the choir. The subjects run in courses from the lowest compartment on the left to the lunette on the right side.

1. THE ENTRANCE OF SAINT AUGUSTINE INTO THE GRAMMAR SCHOOL.

2. ADMISSION OF SAINT AUGUSTINE TO THE UNIVERSITY OF CARTHAGE.

BENOZZO GOZZOLI

3. MONICA PRAYING FOR HER DEPARTING SON.
4. PASSAGE OF SAINT AUGUSTINE FROM AFRICA TO ITALY.
5. RECEPTION OF SAINT AUGUSTINE UPON HIS ARRIVAL.
6. SAINT AUGUSTINE TEACHING AT ROME.
7. DEPARTURE OF THE SAINT FOR MILAN.
8. MEETING OF SAINT AUGUSTINE WITH AMBROSE AT MILAN.
9. SAINT AUGUSTINE HEARS AMBROSE PREACH.
10. SAINT AUGUSTINE READS SAINT PAUL'S EPISTLES.
11. BAPTISM OF SAINT AUGUSTINE BY AMBROSE.
12. SAINT AUGUSTINE VISITS THE HERMITS OF MONTE PISANO.
   He explains the rules of his order ; his vision of the child on the sea shore.
13. DEATH OF SAINT MONICA.

Lunettes.

14. SAINT AUGUSTINE AND HIS CONGREGATION.
15. TRIUMPH OF SAINT AUGUSTINE OVER FORTUNATUS THE MANICHAEN.
16. SAINT AUGUSTINE IN ECSTASY.
17. DEATH OF SAINT AUGUSTINE.

On the front Faces of the Pilasters.

TOBIT AND THE FISH.

ANGEL AND TOBIT

SAINT FINA.

MARTYRDOM OF SAINT SEBASTIAN.

SAINT SEBASTIAN.

SAINT MONICA.

SS. NICHOLAS OF TOLENTINO, NICOLAS OF BARI, ELIAS.

SS. BARTOLUS, GIMIGNANO, AND JOHN THE BAPTIST.
   With a small martyrdom of Saint Bartolus on a lower frieze.

In the Entrance Vaulting.

CHRIST BETWEEN THE APOSTLES AND EVANGELISTS.

In the Chapel of the Holy Sacrament.

PAINTING ON PANEL OF VIRGIN AND CHILD.
   Attributed to Gozzoli

Over the Altar of Saint Sebastian.

SAINT SEBASTIAN PRESERVING THE TOWN OF SAN GIMIGNANO FROM THE PLAGUE IN 1464. Fresco.

PALAZZO PUBBLICO.

In the Sala del Consiglio is a large fresco of the Virgin and Child surrounded by Saints, with Donors, painted in 1317 by Lippo Memmi, and restored in 1467 by Gozzoli.

COLLEGIATA.

THE MARTYRDOM OF SAINT SEBASTIAN, WITH OUR SAVIOUR, THE VIRGIN, AND VARIOUS SAINTS.

Painted between the two entrances. The saints are SS. Anthony the Hermit (with two angels), Augustine, Bernardino of Siena, and Jerome.

THE CRUCIFIXION.

Close to the previous frescoes, bearing the same date, 1465–66.

CHAPEL OF STA. FINA, COLLEGIATA.

VIRGIN AND CHILD, WITH ANGELS ABOVE HOLDING A CROWN AND WREATHS OF FLOWERS, AND SAINTS KNEELING BENEATH.

This large painting on panel, together with eight others by different artists, is now in the choir of Sta. Fina, having been removed from suppressed convents in the neighbourhood.

CONVENT OF MONTE OLIVETO (outside San Gimignano).

CRUCIFIED SAVIOUR AND SAINTS.

A large fresco in the cloister.

CHURCH OF SAN ANDREA (three miles outside San Gimignano).

VIRGIN AND CHILD ENTHRONED, WITH PREDELLA, A RESURRECTION.

In the choir. Formerly in the church of Santa Maria Maddalena.

ROME

MUSEUM OF THE LATERAN.

THE VIRGIN GIVING HER GIRDLE TO SAINT THOMAS.

Formerly in the church of Saint Fortunato, Montefalco.

MUSEUM OF THE VATICAN.

THE MIRACLES OF SAINT HYACINTH.

This is doubtful. Crowe and Cavalcaselle mention that a predella in this gallery "assigned to Gozzoli is by a Ferrarese artist."

CHURCH OF S. MARIA IN ARACOELI.

FRESCO OF SAINT ANTHONY AND TWO ANGELS.

Vasari says that Gozzoli painted a fresco in a niche above the altar of the Cappella Cesarina at Aracoeli in Rome, representing Saint Anthony and two angels, with two donors below. Crowe and Cavalcaselle write, "The heads in this piece are the only heads that are not repainted, and it is true that they reveal Benozzo's hand, as do likewise traces of paintings on the lunettes of the portals."

ENGLAND

London

NATIONAL GALLERY.
> VIRGIN AND CHILD ENTHRONED.
> THE RAPE OF HELEN.

BRITISH MUSEUM.
> SOME DRAWINGS.
> Including the design for the figure of Saint Severus in the fresco of San Francesco at Montefalco.

Windsor

ROYAL COLLECTION.
> DRAWINGS.

Oxford

UNIVERSITY GALLERY.
> THE ANNUNCIATION.
> Referred to by Dr. Von Waagen in 1854.

PRIVATE COLLECTIONS

SIR C. HUBERT H. PARRY, BART., HIGHNAM COURT
> THE ANNUNCIATION.

EARL OF ASHBURNHAM.
> THE ARGONAUTS IN COLCHIS.
> Doubtful.

HENRY WAGNER, ESQ.
> VIRGIN AND CHILD.

IRELAND

Dublin

NATIONAL GALLERY.
> HISTORY OF LUCRETIA.

FRANCE

Paris

The Louvre.

THE TRIUMPH OF SAINT THOMAS AQUINAS.

This was formerly in the cathedral at Pisa, and is mentioned by Vasari. In the upper part, Christ in the Heavens open; beneath him, Saint Paul armed with the sword, Moses carrying the Tables of the Law, and the four Evangelists with their emblems; in the central part, Saint Thomas, in a halo, bearing open books on his knees, is enthroned between Aristotle and Plato; at his feet, felled to the ground, Guillaume de Saint-Amour, the enemy of the orders of mendicant friars. At the bottom of the picture on the left, Pope Alexander IV., attended by his cardinals, presides over the assembly of Agnani; on the right bystanders, amongst whom are Albert the Great and the envoys of Saint Louis.

DECORATION OF AN ALTAR, WITH A PREDELLA AND UPRIGHTS.

This is attributed to Gozzoli, but has also been attributed to Fra Angelico. It was formerly in the church of Saint Girolamo at Fiesole. It consists of (1) centre panel: On a throne, surrounded by angels at prayers, the Virgin sits, wrapped up in a blue cloak and a pink robe, in three-quarters profile to the right; she holds a lily, and the Child upright upon her knees; on the left, Saint Jerome pressing a stone against his breast, Saint Cosmo and Saint Damian; on the right, Saint John the Baptist in ecstasy, Saint Francis clasping his hands, and Saint Laurence leaning on a gridiron; on both sides, angels, in the background, orange-trees and cypresses. (2) Predella: in the centre a Pietà; on the left a martyr, who is on the point of being beheaded, sees, in a dream, Saint Jerome on his bed with two disciples watching, the burial of a monk; on the left, Saint Francis of Assisi upheld by angels, appears to a bishop who works before a desk; the sufferings of Saint Cosmo and Saint Damian witnessed by a terror-stricken crowd. At both ends the armorial bearings of the Medici. (3) Uprights: On the right, Saint Peter, Saint Paul and a monk; on the left, three monks.

AUSTRIA

Vienna

Gallery of the Belvedere.

VIRGIN AND CHILD WORSHIPPED BY SAINTS.

GERMANY

DRESDEN

PINACOTHEK.

THE ANNUNCIATION.
This is doubtful. "The small Annunciation (No. 7) is assigned to the School of Fra Angelico, whereas it should, I think, be described as a feeble work by Benozzo Gozzoli."—Morelli.

BERLIN

OLD MUSEUM.

MADONNA.
A youthful work exhibited (1893) in Room VI. No. 60b. Crowe and Cavalcaselle refer to No. 1165a in the Berlin Museum. "An Annunciation assigned to Gozzoli is a poor but old copy from the same subject by Fra Filippo." This ascription does not appear in the last catalogue.

[Photo, Brogi

RICCARDI PALACE, FLORENCE

THE JOURNEY OF THE MAGI

[Photo, Brogi

THE JOURNEY OF THE MAGI

RICCARDI PALACE, FLORENCE

LORENZO THE MAGNIFICENT
ATTIRED AS ONE OF THE MAGI   RICCARDI PALACE, FLORENCE

THE JOURNEY OF THE MAGI   RICCARDI PALACE, FLORENCE

JOURNEY OF THE MAGI (DETAIL)　　　　　　RICCARDI PALACE, FLORENCE

[*Photo, Brogi*

HEAD OF ONE OF THE MAGI (DETAIL)   RICCARDI PALACE, FLORENCE

JOURNEY OF THE MAGI
RICCARDI PALACE, FLORENCE

[*Photo, Alinari*

JOURNEY OF THE MAGI   RICCARDI PALACE, FLORENCE

PARADISE (I.) FROM THE   RICCARDI PALACE, FLORENCE
JOURNEY OF THE MAGI

RICCARDI PALACE, FLORENCE

PARADISE (DETAIL)

PARADISE (DETAIL)   RICCARDI PALACE, FLORENCE

[Photo, Brogi

RICCARDI PALACE, FLORENCE

PARADISE (DETAIL)

PARADISE (II.)   RICCARDI PALACE, FLORENCE

[*Photo, Brogi*

RICCARDI PALACE, FLORENCE

PARADISE (DETAIL)

PARADISE (DETAIL)   RICCARDI PALACE, FLORENCE

PARADISE (DETAIL)   RICCARDI PALACE, FLORENCE

A PIETÀ   [*Photo, Brogi*

UFFIZI GALLERY, FLORENCE

[Photo, Brogi

UFFIZI GALLERY, FLORENCE

THE VIRGIN AND ST. CATHARINE

ST. ANTONY AND ST. BENEDICT

UFFIZI GALLERY, FLORENCE

[*Photo, Alinari*

THE ANNUNCIATION   CHURCH OF ST. MARTIN A MENSOLA, FLORENCE

[Photo, Brogi

PINACOTECA DI BRERA, MILAN

ST. DOMENIC REVIVING A CHILD KILLED BY A HORSE

[*Photo, Alinari*

THE VIRGIN AND CHILD, WITH SS. PETER, JOHN, JEROME, PAUL

VANNUCCI GALLERY, PERUGIA

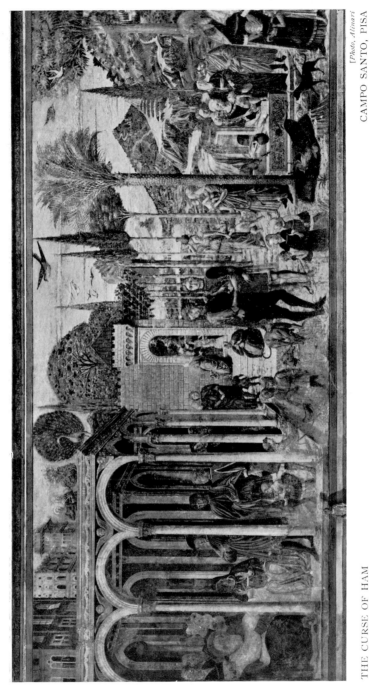

[*Photo, Alinari*

CAMPO SANTO, PISA

THE CURSE OF HAM

24

PORTION OF THE "BUILDING OF THE TOWER OF BABEL."   CAMPO SANTO, PISA

PORTION OF "THE VINTAGE"   CAMPO SANTO, PISA

ABRAHAM AND THE WORSHIPPERS OF BAAL

CAMPO SANTO, PISA

DETAIL OF FRESCO   CAMPO SANTO, PISA

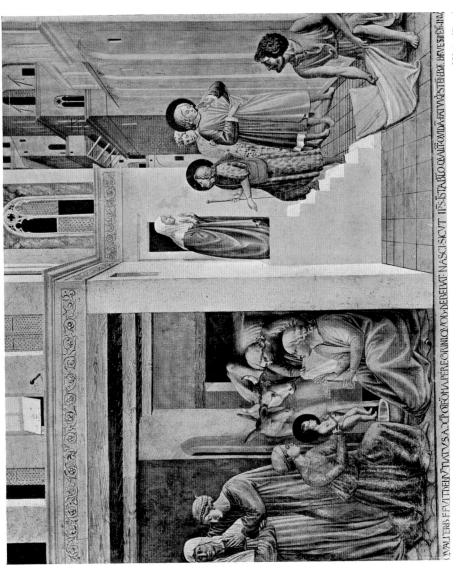

[Photo, Alinari

THE BIRTH, AND INCIDENT OF THE CLOAK THROWN
ON THE GROUND FOR ST. FRANCIS TO WALK ON

CHURCH OF ST. FRANCIS, MONTEFALCO

[*Photo, Alinari*]

ST. FRANCIS GIVES HIS DRESS TO THE
POOR, AND SEES A PALACE IN A DREAM

CHURCH OF ST. FRANCIS, MONTEFALCO

QVALITER·B·F·CORĀ·EPISCOPO·ASISII·RENVIT·PATRI·HEREDITATEM·PATERNAM·ET·ŌNIA·VESTINIENTA·ET·FEMORALIA·PATRI·REIECIT

[*Photo, Alinari*]

ST. FRANCIS PROTECTED FROM HIS FATHER'S
ANGER BY THE BISHOP OF ASSISI

CHURCH OF ST. FRANCIS, MONTEFALCO

QVANDO BEATA VIRGO OSTENT XPO BEATV FRACISCV ET BEATV DOMINICV PROREPARATIONE MVNDI

[Photo, Alinari

MEETING OF ST. FRANCIS AND ST. DOMINIC   CHURCH OF ST. FRANCIS, MONTEFALCO

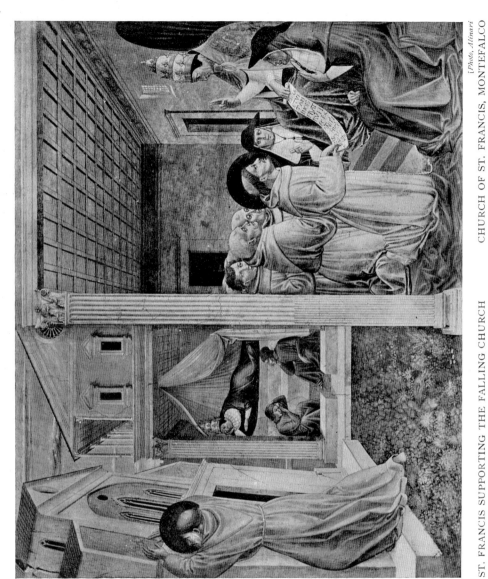

ST. FRANCIS SUPPORTING THE FALLING CHURCH   CHURCH OF ST. FRANCIS, MONTEFALCO

[*Photo, Alinari*]

ST. FRANCIS EXPELLING DEVILS FROM AREZZO   CHURCH OF ST. FRANCIS, MONTEFALCO

THE NATIVITY AT GREGGIO

CHURCH OF ST. FRANCIS, MONTEFALCO

[Photo, Alinari

[Photo, Alinari

ST. FRANCIS BEFORE THE SOLDAN   CHURCH OF ST. FRANCIS, MONTEFALCO

ST. FRANCIS RECEIVING THE STIGMATA   CHURCH OF ST. FRANCIS, MONTEFALCO

THE DEATH OF ST. FRANCIS

CHURCH OF ST. FRANCIS, MONTEFALCO

THE FOUR EVANGELISTS   CEILING OF CHURCH OF ST. FRANCIS, MONTEFALCO

MADONNA AND CHILD,
WITH INCIDENTS FROM THE LIFE OF ST. JEROME

CHURCH OF ST. FRANCIS, MONTEFALCO

[*Photo, Alinari*]

DETAIL OF THE FOREGOING

INCIDENT FROM THE LIFE OF
ST. JEROME (DETAIL)   CHURCH OF ST. FRANCIS, MONTEFALCO

INCIDENT FROM THE LIFE OF
ST. JEROME (DETAIL)

CHURCH OF ST. FRANCIS, MONTEFALCO

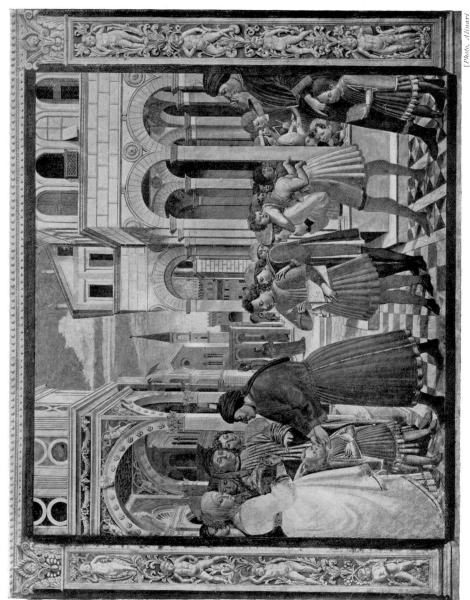

[Photo, Alinari

CHURCH OF ST. AUGUSTINE,
SAN GIMIGNANO

THE ENTRANCE OF ST. AUGUSTINE
INTO THE GRAMMAR SCHOOL

RECEPTION OF ST. AUGUSTINE   CHURCH OF ST. AUGUSTINE
ON HIS ARRIVAL IN ITALY   SAN GIMIGNANO

ST. AUGUSTINE TEACHING IN ROME

CHURCH OF ST. AUGUSTINE, SAN GIMIGNANO

[*Photo, Alinari*

CHURCH OF ST. AUGUSTINE, SAN GIMIGNANO

DEPARTURE OF ST. AUGUSTINE FOR MILAN

[Photo, Alinari

CHURCH OF ST. AUGUSTINE, SAN GIMIGNANO

MEETING OF ST. AUGUSTINE
WITH ST. AMBROSE AT MILAN

ST. AUGUSTINE EXPLAINS
THE EPISTLES OF ST. PAUL

CHURCH OF ST. AUGUSTINE,
SAN GIMIGNANO

BAPTISM OF ST. AUGUSTINE
BY ST. AMBROSE

[*Photo, Alinari*

CHURCH OF ST. AUGUSTINE,
SAN GIMIGNANO

[*Photo, Alinari*]

ST. AUGUSTINE VISITS THE MONKS OF MONTE PISANO   CHURCH OF ST. AUGUSTINE, SAN GIMIGNANO

DEATH OF ST. MONICA

CHURCH OF ST. AUGUSTINE, SAN GIMIGNANO

VEMADMODVM HIERONIMVS PAVLO ANTE
AVGVSTINVM DECELESTI GLORIA INFORMAVIT

[Photo, Alinari

ST. AUGUSTINE IN ECSTACY   CHURCH OF ST. AUGUSTINE, SAN GIMIGNANO

DEATH OF ST. AUGUSTINE

CHURCH OF ST. AUGUSTINE, SAN GIMIGNANO

[Photo, Alinari

ST. SEBASTIAN   CHURCH OF ST. AUGUSTINE, SAN GIMIGNANO

MARTYRDOM OF ST. SEBASTIAN   COLLEGIATE CHURCH, SAN GIMIGNANO

THE VIRGIN AND CHILD WITH
ANGELS AND SAINTS

COLLEGIATE CHURCH, SAN GIMIGNANO

THE VIRGIN GIVING HER
GIRDLE TO ST. THOMAS

MUSEUM OF THE LATERAN, ROME

58

[*Photo, Morelli*]

NATIONAL GALLERY, LONDON

THE RAPE OF HELEN

THE LOUVRE

ALTAR DECORATION

BELVEDERE GALLERY, VIENNA

VIRGIN AND CHILD WORSHIPPED BY SAINTS